THE OTHER HALF OF HISTORY

THE OTHER HALF OF HISTORY

WOMEN

IN

ANCIENT

ROME

Fiona Macdonald

PETER BEDRICK BOOKS
NTC/Contemporary Publishing Group

First published in the United States of America in 2000
by Peter Bedrick Books
a division of NTC/Contemporary Publishing Group
4255 West Touhy Avenue
Lincolnwood (Chicago), Illinois 60712–1975, U.S.A.

Text copyright © Fiona Macdonald 2000
Copyright © Belitha Press Ltd 2000

Series editor: Claire Edwards
Series designer: Jamie Asher
Designer: Zoe Quayle
Picture researcher: Diana Morris
Consultant: Patsy Vanags

Printed and bound in Hong Kong

Library of Congress Cataloging-in-Publication Data
is available from the United States Library of Congress.

Picture acknowledgments:
AAA Collection/© Ronald Sheridan: 11b, 24b. AKG
London: 12l /Erich Lessing: 3r, 32b. Archaeological
Museum, Zara/ET Archive: 21c. Bardo Museum,
Tunis/C. M. Dixon: 26b. Bibliothèque Nationale,
Paris/AKG London/Erich Lessing: 41t. The British
Museum by courtesy of the Trustees: 9br, 14b, 17t,
24tl, 25b /Bridgeman Art Library: 30t/C. M. Dixon: 7cr,
27t, 35t. C. M. Dixon: back cover left, 9t, 10t, 11t, 14c,
15bl, 17b, 19t, 19b, 23t, 23b, 28tr, 29t, 31t, 31c, 34b,
44. ET Archive: front cover cl, 3c, 25c, 45t. Werner
Forman Archive: 10b, 36b. J. Paul Getty Museum,
Malibu/Werner Forman Archive: 7tl. Hereford City
Museum & Art Gallery/Bridgeman Art Library: 15br.
Index/Bridgeman Art Library: back cover tr, 6b, 40b.
Landesmuseum Trier/AKG London /Erich Lessing: 39t
/C. M. Dixon: 33t.

Picture acknowledgments cont.:
Metropolitan Museum, New York/Werner Forman
Archive: 26t. Musée du Louvre/Bridgeman Art
Library: front cover right, 27b, 38b. Musée du
Louvre/RMN/Gérard Blot: 16b. Musée d'Antiquités
Nationales, St. Germain-en-Laye /Bridgeman Art
Library: 37t. Museo Archeologico Nazionale
Napoli/AKG London/Erich Lessing: 3cl, 9bl, 18c, 21b,
28c, 32t, 36c /Bridgeman Art Library: 18b / ET Archive:
1, 7cl, 37b, 43bl, 43tr. Museo del Prado,
Madrid/Bridgeman Art Library: 13t. Museo della
Civiltá Romana/C. M. Dixon: 5b. Museo Gregoriano
Profano, Vatican Museums/Werner Forman Archive:
39b. Museo Nazionale Romano, Roma: C. M. Dixon:
21t, 22b. Museo Ostiense, Ostia/AKG London/Erich
Lessing: 3l, 30b. Museo Prenestino, Roma/ET Archive:
3cr, 29b. Museum of Antiquities of the University and
Society of Antiquaries of Newcastle upon Tyne: 42b.
National Historical Museum, Bucharest/ET Archive: 8b.
National Museum Budapest/C. M. Dixon: front cover
bl, 34t. Private Collection/Bridgeman Art Library: 31b,
33b, 45cr. Spink & Son, London/Bridgeman Art
Library: 4t. Staatsgalerie Stuttgart/AKG London: 12b.
Tullie House Museum & Art Gallery, Carlisle: 20bl.
Vatican Museums/C. M. Dixon: 35b. V&A Museum,
London/ET Archive: 41b.

CONTENTS

The Roman World

The Roman homeland was Italia (now called Italy). From there the Romans conquered a vast empire, stretching from Britain to Spain, North Africa and Turkey. The Roman civilization lasted for more than a thousand years. Roman words, beliefs, ideas and designs still influence many parts of our modern world.

Rome, first and best of cities. Rome, mistress of the world.

MANY POETS WROTE IN PRAISE OF ROME AND ITS EMPIRE

The gold coin above shows Emperor Diocletian, who ruled from AD 284 to 305. Coins were used for trade and to pay the soldiers who guarded the empire. They also carried a message about the emperor's wealth and power.

Heart of the empire

The city of Rome, in central Italy, lay at the heart of the Roman empire. From 31 BC to the fourth century AD, it was the richest, most powerful city in the world. Rome began as a few farmers' huts on two low hills close to the River Tiber. By about 750 BC the settlement had developed into a small town, and by about 300 BC into a busy city. At the height of the Roman empire more than a million people lived in Rome.

By AD 117 the Roman empire included large parts of Europe, North Africa and the Middle East.

Roman empire

Britannia

Germania

Gaul (France)

The Alps

Iberia (Spain)

Italia
Rome •
Pompeii •

Black Sea

Greece

Asia Minor

Carthage •

Mediterranean Sea

AFRICA

Judaea

Alexandria •

Egypt

4

ANCIENT ROME TIME LINE (*c.* is short for *circa* and means *about.*)

c. 1000 BC The first Roman settlement is built on Palatine Hill (Rome stands on seven low hills).

THE AGE OF KINGS
753 BC According to legend, Romulus, the first king of Rome, begins to reign.
509 BC Tarquin the Proud, seventh and last king of Rome, is overthrown by a rebellion.

THE ROMAN REPUBLIC
509 BC

334–264 BC The Romans fight other peoples on the Italian peninsula and win control of most of Italy.
312 BC The Romans carry out large-scale building projects, including an aqueduct bringing fresh water to Rome, and the Via Appia, the first main road leading out of Rome.
218–212 BC Rome and Carthage (a powerful trading city in North Africa) fight for control of the western Mediterranean.
58–51 BC A Roman army, led by Julius Caesar, conquers Gaul (France) and plans to invade Britain.
44 BC Julius Caesar declares himself a dictator, but is murdered by rivals. Civil war follows.

THE ROMAN EMPIRE
27 BC Julius Caesar's heir, Octavian (later known as Augustus), takes control in Rome and becomes the first Roman emperor.
AD 43 The Romans conquer Britain.
AD 64 A fire destroys large areas of Rome. Emperor Nero blames the Christians. Many are persecuted.
AD 79 The volcano Vesuvius erupts, in southern Italy, burying Pompeii and other towns.
AD 98–117 During Emperor Trajan's reign, the Roman empire is at its biggest.
AD 313 Emperor Constantine (who has become a Christian) allows Christians to worship freely. The city of Byzantium (present-day Istanbul) is renamed Constantinople by Emperor Constantine.
AD 395 The Roman empire is divided. The western half is ruled from Rome, the eastern half is ruled from Constantinople (Byzantium).
AD 410 The city of Rome is damaged by invading tribes. The empire begins to collapse.
AD 476 The last emperor in Rome is overthrown. The eastern half of the empire survives and becomes known as the Byzantine empire. It is finally conquered in 1453, by the Ottoman Turks.

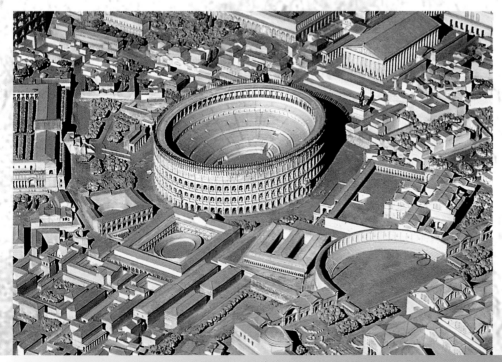

Ancient Rome was a vast city. Its fine buildings, such as the huge Colosseum (center), impressed everyone who traveled there. This model shows what the city would have looked like in about AD 300.

Temples and Treasures

The ancient Romans were famous as builders and engineers, but they also commissioned many works of art. Roman coins, statues, wall paintings, temples and other monuments still survive today. But how much do they tell us about Roman women's lives?

Mythical women

Most great Roman buildings, such as government buildings and temples, were designed by men for men's use. These buildings were often decorated with images of women. The Romans were influenced by ancient Greek art, especially the Greek love of beautiful things. Like the Greeks, Roman artists liked to show images of beautiful young women in wall paintings, statues, and mosaics. These women were often shown as nymphs or goddesses, or as characters from myths and legends. But compared with the Greeks, the Romans also made more pictures of real women in everyday scenes. These were mainly private works of art, such as carvings on tombstones. There are also portrait sculptures of some noble or famous women.

This Roman mosaic picture of a young woman was designed as an image of springtime, not as a portrait of a real person. It was created for a house in Spain, one of Rome's richest provinces.

This portrait shows a Roman woman who lived in Egypt in about AD 170. Pictures like this were kept at home during the person's lifetime, then used to decorate the outside container for their mummified body when they died.

Art for women

Some women worked as professional artists, but most women could only express their artistic likes and dislikes by choosing what to buy, or what to wear. Many pieces of jewelry found at Roman sites were made especially for rich women. From them we can tell that these women liked delicate, expensive designs. Women also asked craftsmen to create other goods such as mirrors and bowls.

The necklace below left is made of gold and mother-of-pearl. It belonged to a wealthy woman from Pompeii, during the first century BC. The other is decorated with a good-luck charm in the shape of a gorgon's head.

Women seen through men's eyes

Women were often painted to be viewed as beautiful objects. Men could gaze at women, but fewer women in paintings are shown looking directly back at men. In many images of husbands and wives, the woman's eyes are turned away, or cast down as a sign of modesty. In fact, this was just a traditional way for artists to show women. We know from writings and carvings that many women, rich and poor, were full of energy, and were practical and intelligent.

Women's own work

At home, women produced many craft objects, especially clothes and household textiles. Female slaves created hairstyles and makeup for their women owners. These were less splendid than buildings or jewelry, but showed that women could be artistic too. Because women usually worked in materials such as linen, wool and silk, many of their creations have long since rotted away, but we can still see their achievements pictured in statues and paintings.

Hidden from History

Compared with many other past civilizations, there is plenty of written evidence to tell us about ancient Rome. Most of this deals with men, but there is writing about women too. In recent years, historians have spent more time studying writing by and about women and what it tells us about women's lives.

Important subjects

Most Roman writers were men. They mainly described people and events that they thought were important. Although some men wrote about powerful, ruling women, men did not usually write about the details of everyday life that made up most women's world. Some Roman men praised, loved and admired women. Others described them with scorn and suspicion. But their descriptions do not tell us what Roman women felt about their own lives.

This young woman had many charming qualities, apart from her youth and beauty. She had a good knowledge of literature, of playing the lyre and of geometry. She was a regular and intelligent listener to lectures on philosophy.

DESCRIPTION OF CORNELIA, A YOUNG WIDOW, AT THE TIME OF HER MARRIAGE TO POMPEY, A FAMOUS ROMAN GENERAL (106–48 BC)

Roman artists and writers dealt with the subjects that interested them—especially wars and politics. This carving shows Roman soldiers crossing a river on a bridge made from ships. It comes from Trajan's column, a tall monument that celebrates men's success in battle.

Business writing

Other sources of written evidence give a less personal view of women. Law codes (made by men) tell us how women were expected to behave. Law court documents tell us what happened when women broke the law. But many documents hardly mention women at all, because women had no legal rights in many areas of public life.

Romans sometimes wrote with pen and ink on parchment scrolls, using ink pots like the ones above. They also used wood or metal to scratch letters on wax or, like Claudia Severa (see box), they wrote in ink on thin slices of wood.

IN HER OWN WORDS

Claudia Severa sends greetings to her friend Lepidina. Sister, please come to visit us on the third day before the Ides of September, to celebrate my birthday. I warmly invite you to come and see us then. It will make the day much more enjoyable for me.

p.s. Sister, I shall expect you! Farewell, my dearest soul. As I hope to live, take care.

This letter is one of many between two Roman women, both army officers' wives. They lived in army forts in northern England around the end of the first century AD. The main part of the letter was dictated, and written by a scribe, but the *p.s.* was added by Claudia Severa herself. It is one of the earliest surviving examples of Roman women's handwriting. Private letters like this show us women's thoughts and feelings. Claudia Severa's letter is warm and friendly. She may even have felt lonely in a northern fort, far from home.

The wall painting (left) shows a woman reading a scroll. She is using a pointer to follow the lines.

WHAT IS A WOMAN ?

Women's Status

By law, a woman was not treated in the same way as a man. Roman laws, and local customs throughout the empire, gave men many rights that women did not have.

Social groups

Roman people were divided into two main groups. The larger was made up of free-born Romans. Members of the smaller group were slaves. There was also a third group, of freedmen and freedwomen. They had once been slaves, but had been set free or bought their freedom. A free woman was better off than a male freedman or a male slave, but did not have equal rights with free men.

This tombstone shows a husband and wife. Although they were not equal in law, many men relied on their wives for practical help, support and advice.

Children all their lives

Of all these groups, only free men could take part in public life and politics. Women could not vote or work in government. In law, they were treated as children. They could not own property, although they could inherit it and pass it on to their husbands or children. Widows had no legal right to their husband's property if there was no will. Women also had no legal control over their own children. They could not take any legal action unless it had been approved by a man.

Some freedwomen became wealthy enough to pay for fine memorials, like this one from Pompeii.

Guardians

Every woman had a male guardian, usually her father or her husband. He had the power to approve or forbid her actions. As head of a family, a husband and father had control of his wife, his children, his son's children and his slaves. If a woman's husband or father died, she could not become head of the family. Her new guardian was usually a male relative —a brother, uncle or cousin—but it could be a complete stranger, appointed by the court. A girl's guardian had to arrange her marriage and look after any property set aside for her dowry. But a woman could complain to the courts if she felt her guardian was being unfair.

Although women had few legal powers, older Roman women could inspire great respect, as this statue shows. The woman has an air of great wisdom and authority.

Mothers and matrons

As a general rule, the Romans thought that having too many children was a sign of uncontrolled passion in women. On the other hand women often earned respect from society in their role as wise and devoted mothers. During the early Empire period, mothers who had three children or more were treated with extra respect, because the population of Rome was falling. Although women did not have the same civil rights as men, in reality older married women were listened to for their intelligence and good sense. The name *Matrona*, which means "mother of a family," became a general title of respect for women.

Romans showed the power of men in government and law in carvings like this one of Roman senators. Senators were important male Roman citizens who gave advice to government officials.

Roman Heroines

Roman writers singled out certain women for praise or blame. By looking at the lives of women they admired, we can find out what Roman men thought a good woman should be.

Judged like men

Roman men admired women. They thought that bringing up children was a noble task. But they also thought that women's goodness was less worthy of respect than men's. Traditionally, Roman men won respect for three qualities: faithfulness to family and country (*fides*), respect for the gods and the laws (*pietas*), and manliness, shown by courage, strength and skill (*virtus*). These were the most noble qualities. The best Roman women should try to copy them.

A brave heroine

Cloelia was one of the only women to be honored by a statue in the Forum at Rome. It was for courage and endurance, skills usually admired in men. In 507 BC, when Rome was at war, she swam the fast-flowing River Tiber to rescue women captured by enemy soldiers, and led them to safety.

The nineteenth-century painting above shows the famous Roman heroine Cloelia swimming the River Tiber with women she had rescued.

The artist in this painting has shown a woman offering Cornelia jewelry, to remind people that Cornelia valued her sons more than her own wealth or appearance.

12

Stories of heroic Roman women were still being enjoyed in books and paintings hundreds of years after Roman times. This painting shows Lucretia's suicide.

An ideal mother

Cornelia lived during the second century AD, and belonged to a noble family. She won fame as the ideal selfless mother. She had 12 children, but only two, Tiberius and Gaius, survived. She brought them up to have the highest standards of honesty and justice, and once described them as her only jewels. The brothers began a series of social reforms, but Tiberius was murdered and Gaius was forced to commit suicide.

Death rather than shame

Lucretia was the wife of a Roman army commander. She was beautiful, faithful and modest. In 509 BC she was raped by the son of the tyrannical king of Rome. She made her husband and father promise to seek revenge, then killed herself. In Roman times, if a woman was raped, she was seen as a ruined woman. The Romans honored Lucretia because she chose death rather than bring shame to her family.

LIVING FOR OTHERS

The best sort of woman will be manly and cleanse herself of cowardice so that she will not be overcome by suffering or fear.

MUSONIUS, PHILOSOPHER AND WRITER (AD 30–101)

In about AD 100, the philosopher Musonius described his idea of a good woman. His was a typical view of the time. Musonius thought that a woman's most important duties were to run the household and be faithful to her husband. She should not spend too much money, or worry too much about her appearance. Women should be honest and never greedy. They should not seek fame or praise, and never be angry or quarrel. They should also love their children 'more than their own life'.

Love and Marriage

Marriage was almost certainly the most important event in most Roman women's lives. Where they lived and who they spent their lives with depended upon it. Yet they had very little power to decide who they married. This was especially true if they were wealthy and free-born, because marriage was often used to link families together in strong alliances.

If we could survive without a wife, citizens of Rome, all of us would do without that nuisance, but since nature has so decreed that we cannot manage comfortably with them, nor live in any way without them, we must plan for our lasting preservation rather than our temporary pleasure.

QUINTUS CAECILIUS METELLUS MACEDONICUS, 131 BC

A betrothal was a legal promise to marry at a later date. This betrothal ring is decorated with clasped hands—the sign of a binding agreement.

Roman weddings like the one below took place in the bride's home. Afterward, the bride was led to the groom's home, where he carried her over the threshold. Brides wore long robes and a bright orange veil.

A practical arrangement

For most men, marriage was a practical arrangement. Female slaves could cook and clean, but only a wife could give birth to children who would continue the family name, inherit property and link with the spirits of dead ancestors. Many couples did grow to love one another dearly too. Some men lived with women without marrying them. These women were known as concubines. This was an accepted way for men, such as soldiers, whose jobs did not allow them to marry, to have a family life. But their children had no legal rights.

14

Arranged by families

Marriages were arranged by families. Parents might try to find a rich bride for their son, or arrange a marriage between their daughter and a powerful politician, hoping to win favors and gain political influence. Usually a bride's family gave her future husband a dowry, made up of land, goods or money. Girls could marry as young as 12 years old. The legal age for boys to marry was 14, although many men waited until they were 30 or more.

Slave "wives"

Slaves were not allowed to marry, but many slave women formed relationships with slave men. These couples called one another husband or wife, and their friends treated them as if they were legally married. But they had no rights. Owners could sell one of the partners at any time, or send them away, or sell their children.

The Romans worshiped Venus, goddess of love. She was helped by her son Cupid, who shot arrows of love to make people fall in love with each other. Cupid is shown on the left in this Roman marble statue.

ST. VALENTINE'S DAY

The modern St. Valentine's Day is based on the ancient Roman festival of Lupercalia, which was celebrated on February 15th. The festival was held to bring fertility to people, animals and crops. As part of the festival young women wrote their names on scraps of parchment and put them into a bowl. Young men picked out a name and asked to be friends with the woman named on it for the coming year.

By about AD 400 Lupercalia was no longer celebrated. But on February 14th Christians honored the memory of St. Valentine, a young man killed for being a Christian. But the old custom did not disappear altogether. Men still asked women to be their girlfriend in mid-February, and the tradition has lasted until today. The Victorian Valentine card below has the motto "faithful and true."

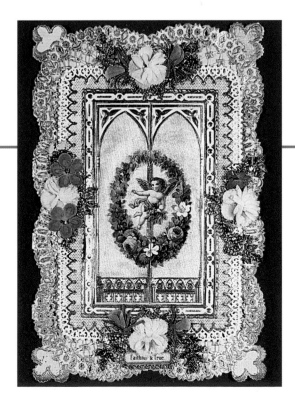

A Girl's Childhood

Not all Roman babies were allowed to survive. Those who were sickly might be killed immediately. Unwanted babies, or babies whom their parents could not afford to feed, were left in public places. They either died, or were adopted by strangers. Some historians think that more girls than boys were left in this way. Children were often left on dung heaps because the rotting rubbish kept the babies warm and helped them to survive. In Roman Egypt, some children were named "born on a dung heap," because they were found there.

I've never seen anyone more cheerful or agreeable or worthy of a long life.... She was just under 14 but was as wise as an old woman.... How she would throw her arms around her father's neck! ... How studiously and intelligently she read, and how sparingly she played....

LETTER BY PLINY THE YOUNGER, MOURNING THE DEATH OF MINICIA MARCELLA, C. AD 105

Children's names

A baby girl was named on the eighth day after her birth. Boys were named on the ninth day. In the Republican era, girls were given the female form of their father's family name (like a modern last name). For example a girl might be called Antonia from her father's name Marcus Antonius. If a family had two or more daughters, then they were called Antonia the elder, and Antonia the younger, or Antonia the second and so on. They might also have a family nickname.

This child's stone tomb shows children playing. The girls are playing a ball game, while the boys are rolling a nut down a wooden board, to knock over a heap of nuts at the bottom.

Dolls were very popular with Roman girls. They often had beautiful clothes and fashionable hairstyles. This is the remains of a rag doll. The body is made of twisted rope.

Education

Many young girls were taught to read and write by their mothers, at home. When they were seven, wealthy girls and boys went to school, or had lessons from a private tutor if their families could afford it. Many girls left school at around 12, the age they could marry. Boys often continued to study at school and university, or were taught by famous scholars. Until they were 12, boys and girls learned the same subjects: reading, writing, math and rhetoric (the art of speaking well and arguing clearly). Some Roman writers thought that if women studied too much, they would become too strong-willed and would neglect their families. Others argued that mothers should be as well-educated as possible, for the good of their children.

Work and play

Girls spent their childhood in very different ways, depending on whether they were slaves or free-born, rich or poor. Girls born into wealthy families spent their time playing and studying. Free-born girls from ordinary families had time to play, but also helped their parents at home, in workshops and on farms. Some might also go to school. Slave girls had to work from the time they reached about five years old. They helped their slave mothers around the house or in the fields, or served as companions to rich free-born girls. When they reached 12 or 13, slave girls might begin to learn a skilled trade.

Sometimes rich men and women asked famous artists to carve portraits of themselves and their children, like this one of a Roman girl. Sometimes such portraits were made in memory of the dead.

17

HEALTH AND BEAUTY

Women's Bodies

Compared with many other cultures, the Romans were very open about sex, but this did not affect their ideas about women's behavior. A Roman girl was expected to be a virgin when she married. Virginity was important because it was linked closely to inheritance and family honor. A Roman man needed to feel sure that his wife's child, especially a son, was really his.

Diana was the goddess of hunting, and the protector of unmarried girls. She is usually shown, as she is below, with her bow and arrow.

The carving above shows a trained midwife (on a stool, left) with a woman giving birth, sitting upright.

A dangerous time

We do not know for certain how many mothers and babies died in childbirth, but it may have been almost one in five. To help them through pregnancy and childbirth, wealthy women hired midwives. Except for a very few women doctors, midwives were the only female health professionals in ancient Rome. Some trained with male doctors, others relied on knowledge passed down from mother to daughter. Most midwives were freedwomen, but a few were slaves.

This carving shows a woman surrounded by medicines in a pharmacy. She would use the pestle (on her right) to grind up herbs and powders in a special bowl called a mortar.

Wet nurses

Wealthy women who survived the dangers of childbirth employed wet nurses to feed and care for their babies. Wet nurses were usually kept on as nannies, and often developed a close bond with the child. Emperor Nero was very fond of his two wet nurses all through his life, and both of them attended his funeral.

Herbs and medicines

Male doctors prescribed many different herbal mixtures to prevent women from becoming pregnant. Some sold love potions, or medicines to cause abortions. These were allowed in early Rome, but later banned by the government. Gentler, safer mixtures were also made and sold by doctors and women herbalists. They included medicines for upset stomachs and creams for rough skin.

THE ROMAN BATHS

The Romans believed that a clean, well-cared-for body was healthy and attractive. Men and women went to the public baths, though usually at different times. Women usually went to the baths in the morning, while men were out at work. At the baths, they cleansed their skin in the hot steam rooms, relaxed in the warm rooms and swam in the cold plunge pool. They could enjoy a massage or beauty treatment, and meet their women friends.

Most Roman towns had at least one public bath. Entrance fees were low, so almost everyone could afford to visit them some of the time. Wealthy families also had their own private baths at home, while ordinary people washed at home in a clay bathtub, wooden bucket or bowl.

These Roman baths were built at the site of a holy spring in the city of Bath, England. The waters were said to have healing powers.

Women and Fashion

Women were responsible for providing clothing for their families. It was the sign of a good woman that she knew how to spin wool or flax and weave her own cloth. Even the Emperor Augustus' wife Livia is said to have woven her husband's warm underwear herself. But most women did not make all the cloth they needed. Wealthy women kept slaves to make cloth for them, and poor women often had no time to spin and weave. They bought their cloth from shops and street markets.

> It would be simpler to count the acorns on an oak tree than to describe all the different hairstyles women wear today.
>
> THE ROMAN POET HORACE, WRITING IN THE FIRST CENTURY AD

Changing fashions

Many Roman women were interested in fashion. They often copied the hairstyles worn by the emperor's wife. Compared with today, styles changed slowly, but there was usually something new and interesting to admire in women's robes, shoes, hairstyles, makeup and jewelry.

Tunics and robes

Roman clothes were designed to cover women from head to foot. Women wore a linen tunic called a *tunica*, which was usually knee-length. Over this they wore a long robe called a *stola*, made of wool or silk, that fastened at the shoulders with metal brooches. Women often draped a shawl, called a *palla*, over their shoulders, which they could pull up over their head. Poor women wore clothes of rough, undyed fabrics, in white, brown or gray. Wealthy women wore softer clothes, dyed in bright colors. Some wore silk cloth imported from China. Under their tunics, women wore linen briefs and a wide strip of linen as a bra. Some women also wore corsets made of leather.

This woman is wearing a long tunica, *with a* stola *over the top. You can just see the* tunica *under the* stola's *hem. She has a* palla *over her shoulders, and she is holding a fan.*

This girl is pouring perfume into a jar. Perfumes were made from flowers, spices and animal scents, mixed with honey, oil or lard. Salt helped to preserve them.

Hairstyles and wigs

Women had long hair, which they tied up in a knot or bun held in place by ribbons and hairpins. Sometimes plain styles were fashionable. At other times women wore their hair braided or curled. For these fashions, a woman needed the help of a skilled slave or hairdresser. If their own hair was not suitable, women wore wigs made from real hair, brought from other countries. Dark hair from India was popular, but long blonde hair, cut from the heads of captured German slaves, was much rarer and highly prized. Some women used a mixture of ash and urine to bleach their own hair.

Cloaks and shoes

For extra warmth in winter, women wore a thick woolen cloak. Indoors, and in hot weather, women and children wore sandals. Sandals were not fashionable for men until about AD 180. Outside, everyone wore closed shoes or tough leather boots to protect their feet from rough and dirty roads.

Roman hairpins were decorated with many designs, such as goddesses and empresses. Some pins were tipped with glass beads or little pieces of gold to create a colorful, sparkling effect.

Makeup and perfume

Many women, rich and poor, used makeup, usually made by their slaves. They lined their eyes with black charcoal, and used yellow saffron, dried berries and chalk to make face powder, rouge and eye shadow.

Inside this case, found in Rome, there is a comb, a mirror, hairpins, earrings, a ring, and a jar to hold ointment or makeup.

21

WOMEN AT HOME

Households, Families and Slaves

For legal and practical reasons, respectable women almost never lived on their own in ancient Roman times. Most women lived their whole lives surrounded by their family, and often by slaves. Because many women spent their lives working at home, the quality of everyday life depended on their home environment.

> Some husbands trap wives with the promise of a little housekeeping money, then condemn them to the continuous hard work and boredom of housework and account-keeping ... and treat them just like servants.
>
> PLUTARCH (AD 46–120) WAS GREEK, BUT VISITED ROME AND WROTE ABOUT ROMAN LIFE.

A Roman household

The Roman word for a household was *familia*. A household included more than just parents, grandparents and children. It included the house and land, plus all the people associated with it. These might include distant relatives, freedmen, freedwomen and slaves.

Father of the household

The head of each Roman household was called the *paterfamilias* (*pater* means father in Latin). The paterfamilias was the senior surviving man in any family. Grown-up sons, even if they were married with children of their own, still remained within his power. The paterfamilias had the power of life and death over all his household. He also controlled what they could and couldn't do. Bad behavior by one member reflected badly on them all. This meant that a woman's character and worth might be judged by how her male relatives behaved.

Every family with enough money kept servants. The male servant (left) is dressed to go outside, perhaps to carry messages or go shopping. The woman servant is wearing indoor clothes, perhaps ready for cooking, cleaning or child care.

Many wealthy Roman houses were designed like this one, with the rooms built around a courtyard. In warm weather women and girls could enjoy fresh air here in private.

High style

The basic structure of a household was the same throughout the empire, but the surroundings in which women lived were not the same. The biggest difference was between rich and poor. Rich households might be made up of hundreds of people, because the wealthiest families owned many slaves. A rich family could afford a large house and beautiful garden. The rooms were filled with expensive furniture and decorated with wall paintings and mosaic floors in the latest style. In Rome, rich people liked to live on hilltops where the air was fresher, and there were good views.

Ordinary homes

An ordinary household usually contained a married couple and their children, the husband's parents (if they were still alive), unmarried aunts and uncles, and, at the most, one or two slaves. An average Roman family probably had two or three children, though more may have been born, and not survived.

City housing

Ordinary living conditions were often cramped, especially in big cities. Some families lived in apartments, which were either part of a larger building, or were specially built high-rise blocks, called *insulae*. In the city of Rome, these crowded homes were always in danger of fire, flood or collapse. Other families lived in rooms behind their businesses. The poorest families hired rooms in houses or above shops, or built huts in back streets. Ordinary people only had simple furniture, such as wooden beds and stools, woolen blankets, pottery dishes and metal cooking pots.

This model shows a block of apartments from Ostia, a port near Rome. Often whole families lived in just one room of a building like this.

Running a Home

The Romans believed that outdoor work was harder than indoor work and more suitable for men than women, because men were physically stronger. In fact housewives and women slaves also worked hard, running family households.

The senior woman in each household usually kept the keys of the house. She was responsible for locking chests, cellars and storehouses. This Roman key is made of bronze.

Managing a household

Households were owned and controlled by men, but they were usually managed by women. Most domestic slaves were women too. They carried out everyday tasks, such as shopping at markets and stalls, cooking, cleaning, doing the laundry, looking after the kitchen garden, and fetching water from the public fountain or well. A rich, free-born woman would not do physical work like this herself, but organized slaves to do it for her. Women from families who could not afford slaves had to do all the hard domestic work themselves.

Vesta was the Roman name for the Greek goddess of the hearth. (The Greeks called her Hestia.) She represented the safety and welcome that women were expected to provide in their homes. Here Vesta is shown with an offering of a plate of cooked food.

Hard labor

Without clean water on tap and modern machines, many chores, such as washing dishes, sweeping and scrubbing floors, or cleaning and lighting fires, were dirty and exhausting. In wealthy houses, there were also glass windows to clean, and pewter and silver dishes to polish. After dark, most Roman houses were lit by oil-burning lamps. They needed constant attention—trimming the wick and keeping them filled with olive oil—to make sure that they did not produce dirty clouds of smoke, go out, or set the house on fire. Women were responsible for all these chores.

This oil lamp is made of gold. It was made as an offering to the gods. Ordinary oil lamps were similar, but made of pottery or bronze.

Washing and drying

Washing clothes was another major task. Dirty laundry was taken to a nearby stream, or washed in buckets in kitchens or courtyards. Roman clothes were made from many yards of fabric. When they were wet they became very heavy. Clothes were washed in cold water, using lye (an early form of soap, made from wood-ash). This roughened and cracked the hands of the laundry slaves. Washing was hung from trees or draped over bushes to dry. Creases were removed by rubbing dried clothes with a rounded stone or smooth glass. Washing was then pressed in a clothes press. In Pompeii, a center for the textile industry, women often took their clothes to professional laundries to be washed.

WHO'S IN CHARGE?

A Roman woman's place within the household changed during her lifetime. A young bride who went to live in her husband's family home had to help and obey her mother-in-law, who ran the household. When the new wife had children, her status rose, especially if they were sons. Her status rose again when her mother-in-law became old or ill and after she died.

But some young women had homes of their own. Some poor families had no room to house their married children, so young couples rented cheap rooms or built shacks of their own. And, because many Roman women did not live more than 50 years, some mothers died before their sons were married, and the new wife was left in charge.

Floors and clothes were scrubbed clean with scrubbing brushes, like this one made of wood and animal bristles.

In the Country

Some wealthy Romans owned a town house, and a villa in the country too, surrounded by an estate made up of farmland and woods. Families moved to the villa during the summer, to escape the heat of the city, with its smells, dirt and noise. The farm was run all year round by a farm manager. In some parts of the empire, villas were occupied by government officials, who ruled lands conquered by Rome.

Rich villas had painted walls and fine furniture, like this couch, decorated with ivory, glass and semiprecious stones. Men and women sat or lay on couches, eating food set out on low tables.

In this mosaic of a Roman villa, people are gardening, looking after flocks and herds, hunting and catching birds to eat. At the bottom of the picture, servants are presenting their offerings to the master and mistress of the villa.

Organizing and entertaining

When the head of a family decided to visit his country villa, his wife sent instructions to the villa's slaves to prepare for their arrival. Once there, she inspected the rooms and storerooms, and gave orders for meals, household repairs and extra housework. She might discuss plans for new gardens or for redecorating rooms with craftsmen and senior slaves. A wife spent much of her time supporting her husband, by acting as a hostess to important local people. In remote parts of the empire, where rebellions were always a danger, this required intelligence and tact. In the lands closer to Rome, it might help her husband in his political career.

These decorated spoons made of gold and silver have dolphin-shaped handles. They may have been used to serve wine mixed with water, or to eat stew. (The Romans did not have forks.)

Army wives

Until AD 197, only senior army officers were allowed to marry. When officers were posted abroad, their wives often chose to go with them, taking their children and slaves as well. These women had to organize for their household belongings to be taken to their new home, or else set up a new home in an unfamiliar land. They had to cope with new surroundings, an unknown language and strange food. Sometimes there was also the danger of enemy attack.

Unofficial wives

Concubines of ordinary soldiers (see page 14) also followed them on campaigns. They lived in settlements outside the fort walls, and earned money by cooking, mending, washing, and brewing beer. They hoped to marry their partners once they retired from the army—if their men were not killed in battle first.

FORT WOMEN

For safety, army wives lived inside a fort. A large fort had different groups of buildings. The fort commander and his wife lived in a comfortable house, with a kitchen, a bathroom, and central heating. Centurions and their families lived in two or three small rooms at the end of a barrack block.

There were usually only a few wives at a fort, and, because they came from different backgrounds, they could not mix socially. Commanders' wives, especially, must often have felt lonely (see page 9). They relied on their children or female servants for company. A few women found unexpected ways of occupying their time. For example senators in AD 21 were upset by a report that a woman called Plancina had commanded battle practice.

Julia Domna (died AD 217) traveled to different parts of the Roman empire with her husband, Emperor Septimus Severus. Wherever she stayed she became a leader of fashion. She also invited scholars to visit the court to discuss their ideas. After her husband died, one of her two sons murdered the other, and Julia ran the government in Rome on her surviving son's behalf.

Food and Drink

Roman people liked to eat well-cooked, highly spiced food. Roman cook books included dishes made from rare and expensive ingredients, such as larks' tongues, peacocks and dormice. This kind of food was only prepared for rich people, or on special occasions. Ordinary people ate simpler foods. They also bought take-out snacks from taverns and stalls.

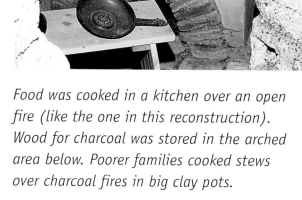

Food was cooked in a kitchen over an open fire (like the one in this reconstruction). Wood for charcoal was stored in the arched area below. Poorer families cooked stews over charcoal fires in big clay pots.

Sugar was almost unknown in Roman lands. But Romans enjoyed sweet fruits, such as these grapes, apples, pomegranates and figs.

Preparing meals

Wealthy wives employed a female housekeeper to run their kitchen and arrange for fetching and storing food supplies. Cooks in ordinary houses were usually women, but the best-known cooks, in rich homes, were men. Male and female slaves were sent to the market to buy food. If the family owned a country villa, much of the food they ate was grown on their own estate. In poorer families, housewives shopped and cooked in addition to their other chores.

Three meals a day

The Romans ate three meals a day. Breakfast was a simple snack of bread and cheese, or just bread and water. Lunch was a light meal of cold meat, bread, vegetables and fruit. The main meal of the day was dinner, when families and friends sat down together at the end of a day's work. For most families, dinner was a plain but hot meal of bean or lentil soup or stew, with bread and vegetables. This might be followed by fruits, nuts and honey.

Different diets

Historians have studied skeletons from Roman burials and found that women's teeth were less decayed than men's. This might mean that women drank less wine and ate less fat, honey and sticky dried fruit than men. This was probably because women were not seen as important and were not offered the richest food.

Wine and water

All Romans liked to drink wine with their dinner, usually mixed with water. Women were not supposed to drink too much or lose control of themselves. Traditional stories told how a Roman husband killed his wife when he discovered her drunk, and the courts did not find him guilty of murder.

Dinner parties

Wealthy families often held large dinner parties. There were many courses of the most delicious food. It was an honor to be invited, and could help ambitious men with their career. Although these dinner parties were seen as part of the male world of business and politics, respectable married women were invited to them, and proved they could match men in lively, witty conversation.

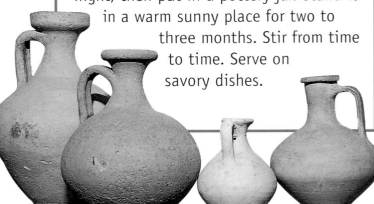

RECIPE

Favorite Fish Sauce

Take sprats, anchovies or mackerel. Add lots of salt and mix well. Leave one night, then put in a pottery jar. Stand it in a warm sunny place for two to three months. Stir from time to time. Serve on savory dishes.

Pottery jars were used to store oil, vinegar and wine. Other pottery containers were used to store goods such as flour, to keep them safe from rats and mice.

In this mosaic of an outdoor banquet, men and women sit on couches and are entertained by a woman musician.

WOMEN AND WORK

Businesswomen

Many women from ordinary free-born families had to work, to earn money. They were not allowed to train for careers such as medicine or law, so most women's jobs were simple ones, and poorly paid. Jobs were usually based on traditional female skills, such as cooking or child care, and many women worked in the weaving trade.

Working together

Although jobs and training were mostly for men, wives sometimes worked alongside their husbands. They were able to combine a craft or trade with their housework and child care because many businesses were based in family homes. Women's help with a family business became vital if their husbands fell ill or were injured, or were simply lazy.

A helping hand

A craftworker's wife might help to prepare raw materials, or pack finished goods. A shopkeeper's wife might help buy and sell, or keep accounts. The wives of fishermen or vegetable growers would salt and dry fish, or sell vegetables at local markets.

Food stalls were often run by women. This one has two pet monkeys, probably to attract customers. Fresh chickens are hanging up, and there are live hares in cages below the counter.

Many husbands and wives worked as business partners. Here the husband is chopping meat in his butcher shop, while his wife does the accounts.

Useful services

In towns there were more jobs open to women, providing goods and services for people living or visiting there. In Pompeii there were women tavern owners, waitresses, bakers, weavers, moneylenders and laundresses. In Ostia, a port near Rome, there were women shoemakers, doctors, nurses and barmaids. Women also worked as wet nurses, children's nurses, midwives and public bath attendants in every Roman town.

Professionals

Many slave owners freed their women slaves and helped set them up in business. Slaves used the skills they had learned in wealthy households, such as spinning, weaving, hairdressing and midwifery. A few managed to train for jobs normally closed to women and became doctors or librarians. In some parts of the empire, such as Gaul, skilled freedwomen organized themselves into women's guilds. These guilds offered training, and support in hard times.

EUMACHIA OF POMPEII

Eumachia, daughter of Lucius, in her own name and that of her son, Marcus, built a porch and covered colonnade, dedicated to peace and piety, at her own expense....

TEXT ON A PLAQUE AT THE FORUM IN POMPEII.

Eumachia lived in Pompeii in the first century AD. She was the daughter of an important citizen, and also a successful businesswoman. She used her money to build a fine new covered hall at the forum in Pompeii, as a gift to the citizens. Here traders could set up their stalls and be sheltered from the sun. Her statue (left) was set up at the back of the hall by cloth workers.

The Street of Tombs in Pompeii, painted in 1855 by a German artist, was where important people in Pompeii were buried. Eumachia's tomb was the largest in the street—a sign of her wealth and importance.

Entertainment

Some Roman women went out to work as entertainers, but they were not accepted by respectable society. High-ranking men were not supposed to marry them, although one emperor married a former actress who was the daughter of a performing-bear keeper. Women entertainers often came from families who already worked in the theater as singers, dancers or actors. Others came from poor families, but hoped to find fame and fortune by working on the stage.

Respectable women only played music in their own homes to their family and friends. In the painting above, a woman is playing the kithara, a popular stringed instrument.

After work

Many respectable, wealthy women learned singing, and how to play the harp and the lyre. They played at home to entertain their families. Wealthy women read poetry, listened to music and puzzled over board games. They enjoyed going to the theater and watching chariot races. Women were also allowed to go to amphitheaters to see gladiator fights and wild-beast hunts, but they had to sit in seats at the back.

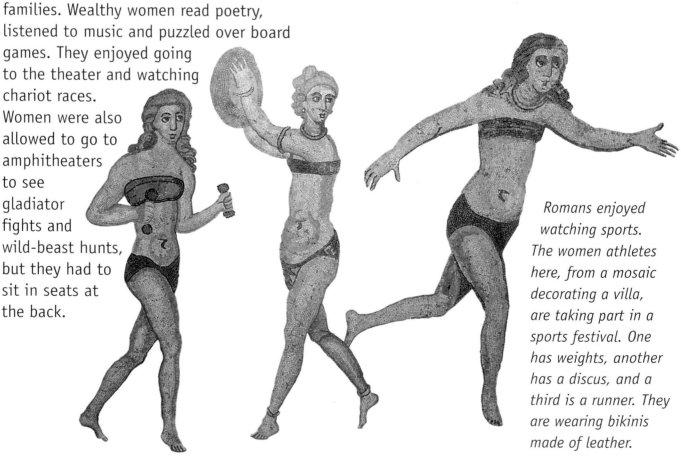

Romans enjoyed watching sports. The women athletes here, from a mosaic decorating a villa, are taking part in a sports festival. One has weights, another has a discus, and a third is a runner. They are wearing bikinis made of leather.

32

Romans often gave their slaves Greek names, to show that they were not real Roman citizens. On the mosaic above, Eleni is shown dancing to entertain guests at a Roman banquet.

Women in the theater

All big cities and many towns had theaters. Some had permanent actors, others were visited by traveling players. Many plays were new, written to comment on the latest events. Others were old favorites. Most plays included music and dance, and in some the audience had to sing along and shout, hiss and boo. Actresses performed in all kinds of plays, but the most important parts were played by men. Men and women actors wore masks on their faces, so that their character's expression could be seen clearly from the back of the theater.

Struggling to survive

Many women worked as prostitutes. They all had to register with government officials, and pay a tax. Few chose this way of life. Many were slaves bought at auctions by male or female brothel-keepers. Others were desperate to make a living in any way they could find. They may have been left by their husbands, or were cast-off concubines, or runaway slaves. Brothels earned a lot of money for their owners, but few prostitutes became rich themselves.

Music and dance

Some slaves were trained in mime, music and dancing, and were expected to entertain their owners' guests at dinner parties, as well as serve their food. Professional female dancers, singers and acrobats also performed in theaters and could be hired for dinner parties. As one Roman wrote, "No dinner is complete without wine, wit and the company of a lovely girl."

This wall painting shows a man and woman's face in the typical style of Roman theater masks.

WOMEN AND RELIGION

Public Worship

Religion played an important part in Roman people's lives. They attended public religious ceremonies and also worshiped in small groups at home, or joined new, foreign cults. Women played their own role in all these different ways of worshiping.

This mask is of the goddess Juno. Married women prayed to her for protection, and took flowers to her temple. Husbands also prayed to Juno to bring their wives good health.

Gods and goddesses

The Romans worshiped a family of gods, headed by Jupiter, lord of the sky. The most important goddesses were Juno (Jupiter's wife), Minerva (goddess of wisdom), Diana (goddess of hunting) and Ceres (goddess of harvest and plenty). Gods and goddesses protected the community and helped it in difficult times, such as famine, warfare or plague. In return, the Romans honored them with processions, gifts and sacrifices.

Public ceremonies

Religious ceremonies were supposed to encourage good behavior in Roman citizens. Both men and women could serve as priests and priestesses, but there were fewer priestesses. They were chosen from the oldest, most important families in Rome. They took part in temple ceremonies, where they said prayers and made offerings on behalf of all citizens in Rome.

This statue shows a priestess taking part in a temple ceremony. In one hand she is holding a pot of incense, to fill the temple with sweet-smelling smoke. In the other she is holding a bowl, to pour offerings of wine.

34

Many cities had their own guardian goddesses. The seven gods and goddesses who guard the days of the week are supported on the wings of this city guardian.

VESTAL VIRGINS

The vestal virgins were important priestesses in the city of Rome. It was their task to keep a sacred fire burning all the time in the Temple of Vesta, goddess of the hearth (see page 24). The temple stood in the Forum in Rome. Legends told how Rome's power would collapse if the fire were ever to go out. The vestals also had to bake the holy bread used in temple ceremonies.

Vestal virgins were chosen from the daughters of important free-born families when they were about six years old. They were led to the temple by a priest, their hair was cut short, and they were dressed in white, with a veil. They spent ten years training, ten years performing temple rituals, and ten years teaching the young girls who would be priestesses after them. After 30 years of duty, they were free to leave the temple, but few did. It was the only life they had known. If any vestal broke her vow of virginity, she was buried alive.

Victory and peace

The Romans made goddesses out of qualities, such as victory, peace or good luck. They also honored the guardians of cities, such as Roma, the female spirit of their capital city. From the first century AD, the Roman government ruled that dead emperors (and sometimes their wives) should also be worshiped as gods.

Breaking the rules

Sometimes women took part in special women-only ceremonies, such as the festival of *Bona Dea* (the goddess of healing and fertility), which was held once a year. This was held in the house of one of the magistrates, and led by his mother or wife. She made a blood-offering at an altar where a real snake sat on a throne. Then there was wild music, feasting and dancing. By breaking the usual rules of female behavior, this ceremony may have reminded people of how a respectable woman should behave.

Here, three vestal virgins are shown helping priests at a state sacrifice. One of their tasks was to sprinkle sacrificed animals with flour and salt.

Private Worship

Everyday worship was based at home. Each family worshiped the *lares* (household gods) and *penates* (gods of the store-cupboard) by saying prayers and leaving offerings at a family shrine. Men usually led the prayers, but women prepared offerings of food for the shrine and decorated it with flowers on festival days.

...wild fig trees, uprooted from tombs, funeral cypress trees, eggs dipped in the blood of foul frogs, a night owl's feather, herbs from Iolchus and Spain with its rich poisons, and bones torn from the mouth of a hungry bitch....

PART OF THE RECIPE FOR A WITCHES' LOVE POTION, REPORTED BY A ROMAN AUTHOR.

Family prayers

The Romans also respected their ancestors. Twice a year, in February and May, there were special ceremonies linking living family members with the dead. The tombs of dead relatives were cleaned and decorated, and the family gathered there for a solemn meal. Once they were married, women honored their husband's ancestors, not their own.

Many houses had shrines. These were usually filled with little statues of family ancestors made of wood and wax, like the ones below.

Priests and priestesses of Isis often led ceremonies together as equals.

New religions

Many women became followers of new religions, brought to Rome from conquered lands in North Africa and the Middle East after about 150 BC. One of the most popular was the cult of Isis, the Egyptian goddess of life and rebirth. Worship was based on a person's own hopes and prayers, rather than on organized ceremonies. Followers of Isis formed their own community, where women were treated equally with men. Worship was usually led by priestesses, though male worshipers and priests were allowed.

The Celts worshiped many goddesses, including Epona, who protected horses, riders and travelers.

Local traditions

Throughout the empire, there were groups of people who continued to follow their own religious customs. One Roman writer describes a group of black-robed women in Wales with "wild hair, like Furies, brandishing torches." They may have been Druid (Celtic) priestesses, members of an ancient religion banned by the Roman conquerors of Britain.

Superstitions and spells

In ancient Roman times, most people were superstitious. For instance, it was bad luck for a person to sneeze. To protect themselves, men and women often carried or wore lucky charms. Witchcraft was against the law, but most people believed in it, and feared that some women had frightening magic powers. Roman writers left descriptions of witches' spells and rituals, but it is impossible to know how much of these descriptions is true.

CURSES!

Besides taking part in temple ceremonies, saying prayers, and making offerings, Roman people often asked a favorite god or goddess to help them, or to punish someone they did not like. They wrote their requests or curses on thin sheets of lead, as miniature messages, and left them at holy sites. This curse was found in London:

I curse Tretia Maria and her life and mind and memory and liver and lungs mixed together, and her words, thoughts and memory....

Because the lead is damaged, we don't know who wrote this curse, or why they were so angry with Tretia Maria.

In Roman times people thought it was good luck to see a snake. Snakes were also honored as spirits that guarded places. Pictures of snakes were often used to decorate walls and floors.

Death and the Afterlife

Most Romans lived shorter lives than European men and women today, and would have been more familiar with death. Roman beliefs about death and what happened afterward changed over the years, as the Romans came into contact with the different faiths of many peoples.

The Romans borrowed many ancient Greek myths to add to their own. Myths often described people making the terrifying journey between the worlds of the living and the dead. In this carving Orpheus (left) has gone to the Underworld to rescue his dead wife, Eurydice. He finds her spirit there, but fails to bring it back to the living world.

ZETVS   ANTIOPA   AM HION

Life after death

Traditionally Romans believed that a man or woman's spirit survived after death and was carried to a shadowy Underworld, where it became weak and pale. To survive, a spirit had to be remembered by its family and friends. Some Roman tombstones had messages on them to passers-by, such as "Stranger, speak my name—so that I may continue to live."

Burials and funerals

Roman burial customs changed over the years, but this was more a matter of fashion than belief. Women were often buried with objects that surrounded them during their life, such as jewelry, perfumes, spinning and weaving equipment, oil lamps and kitchen pots. Families often paid for carved tombstones as well. Unmarried women who had no family to bury them joined burial guilds. They saved enough for burials and carried out the funeral rites for one another.

Families shared a funeral meal when someone died, like this one carved on a tombstone. Women also prepared meals for feasts in honor of the family (including those who had died) on special days of the year, such as Parentalia in February.

After the funeral

Funerals for men and women were the same, but customs for mourning them were different. Full mourning lasted nine days. It continued, at a lesser level, for one year for a parent or child over six and for one month for a child under six. A wife mourned her husband for ten months. While they were in mourning, women could not go to dinner parties, or wear jewels or purple clothes. If people thought a widow remarried too soon, she had to sacrifice a pregnant cow to the gods. This was a very expensive fine.

Last journey

A dead person was washed and dressed at home by undertakers or slaves. The body was surrounded by sweet-smelling herbs and spices. In Rome and many other parts of the empire, people were buried outside the city. The body was carried, usually at night, in a long funeral procession to the funeral fire or burial ground.

This scene on a family tomb shows women laying out the dead body, while family mourners gather round. Women were usually buried in, or close to, their husband's family tomb.

Music and mourning

A funeral procession was led by musicians playing trumpets. Then came the men, weeping and beating their breasts. Female relatives were followed by professional mourners, who were nearly always women. These mourners sang praises to the dead person. When the procession reached the burial ground, a male relative made a speech, and a professional mourner sang a sad song. Romans usually wore black clothes for funerals, though a few women dressed in white. Women let their hair flow loose, but men covered their heads.

New Beliefs, New Laws

Christianity began in Judaea, a province of the Roman empire. It developed from the teachings of Jesus Christ, a religious leader executed by the Romans in about AD 30. Until AD 313, Christianity was banned, and the punishment for following it was imprisonment and death.

A personal god

One Roman writer described Christianity as "the religion of women, children and slaves." In fact Christianity attracted several rich people, including Emperor Constantine (AD 306–337), but most early followers were fairly powerless people, such as women, slaves and the poor. This may have been because Christianity comforted people whose lives were hard. They believed that God would take care of them, like a loving father. Christians also believed they would enjoy a better life after death. This contrasted with Roman state religion, which aimed to support a well-run society in this world.

Women's role in the Church

Christianity brought companionship to many people. It allowed respectable Roman women to meet others, by going to services and organizing prayer groups. Early Christian leaders disagreed on the role women should have in the new Church. Some thought women should stay at home as wives or nuns, and pray. Others, like St. Jerome, encouraged rich women to use their money to build churches, schools and houses where communities of Christians could live. A few women spoke out about their faith in public, and were punished or killed for their beliefs.

Many Roman rooms were decorated with mosaics of food and animals, but this mosaic carries an extra religious message. Fish and bread were both Christian symbols.

St. Helena was the mother of Emperor Constantine and lived in the fourth century AD. Stories told how she was sent by God to Jerusalem to find the remains of the Cross. She did so, and built a church on the site. This carving shows Jesus on the Cross, with his mother Mary and St. John. The small figures at the bottom are Constantine and St. Helena.

Obedience

Christian leaders taught that it was a woman's duty to be obedient to her husband, even if he treated her badly. (Roman law let wives divorce husbands for some crimes.) They also taught that birth control and abortion were wrong (both were practiced in pre-Christian Rome). Male Church leaders criticized women's love of fashionable clothes, makeup and jewels, saying that such things were gateways to hell.

A pure life

Other Church rules gave women power to control their own bodies for the first time in their lives. These rules encouraged women to live apart from men, so that they could be closer to God. Some women decided not to marry, or to leave their husbands in order to live a pure life

The Romans tried to kill St. Catherine by breaking her bones on a wheel, but the wheel broke. This was seen as a sign from God. St. Catherine is usually shown, as here, with her broken wheel.

SAINT CATHERINE

Catherine lived in Alexandria, in Egypt, in the fourth century AD. The city was part of the Roman empire and a great center of learning. Catherine came from a noble family and was very well educated. She was a Christian at a time when it was against the law. When she was 18 years old, she tried to argue with the emperor that the Christian faith was the only true religion. He was angry and put Catherine in prison. The emperor's wife visited her there, and was so impressed by Catherine, she became a Christian too. After this, the emperor had Catherine beheaded, and she was made a saint by Christian Church leaders.

FAMOUS WOMEN

Scholars and Artists

Roman women from wealthy families were educated in literature, music and philosophy, so that they would be more attractive to their husbands, and good companions. They were not expected to use these skills to earn a living. But some women did give money to help support male scholars, writers, musicians and artists. And a few women managed to break society's rules and win fame for their own wisdom, learning and skill.

Here is the statue of Scholastica, a woman who was pious and very wise. She gave a great sum in gold to rebuild the public baths that had fallen down.

INSCRIPTION ON A PUBLIC MONUMENT

Doctor Fabiola (died in AD 399)

Fabiola was born into a noble family in Rome, and was married, unhappily, while still a teenager. She became a Christian, and later married again, but her husband died. She decided to spend the rest of her life working in medicine and charity. In AD 390, with two friends, she founded a hospital in the port of Ostia, near Rome. She was a skilled surgeon, and admired for the loving care she gave to patients. Another medical woman, who worked alongside her doctor husband (*c.* AD 100), was called Panthia. After her death, he wrote, "Though you were a woman, you were not behind me in skill."

Hypatia (*c.* AD 370–415)

Hypatia lived in Alexandria, the most important city in Roman Egypt and a great center of learning. Her father was a mathematician, and he sent her to study with the greatest scholars of the day. She taught math and philosophy at the University of Alexandria, and wrote books on math and science. These were praised when they appeared, but have not survived for us to read today. Although Hypatia was a respected teacher, her scientific views were criticized by the leader of the Christian Church in Alexandria. He encouraged a mob of men to attack and kill her.

This pottery jug, with a spout, was used for feeding invalids with liquid food. Panthia and Fabiola would have used such items to care for their patients.

Iaia of Cyzicus (*c.* 100 BC)

We know of only eight women who worked as artists during Roman times. Most were the daughters of male artists, and their fathers taught them how to paint. This was the only way they could train professionally. Iaia was described as the daughter and student of her father. She carved ivory, and painted pictures on plaster and wood. She mainly painted women but, unlike many male artists, did not always choose young, rich or beautiful people as her subjects. Her most famous work was of an old woman, but it has not survived. Her work was highly praised, and she was able to ask higher prices for her pictures than many male artists.

We do not know who created this wall painting from Pompeii. It shows a woman artist at work and may even be a self-portrait.

This painting from Pompeii shows a young girl who might be a poet or writer. She is holding a metal stylus in one hand. In her other hand she is holding a wooden writing tablet. A stylus was used to scratch letters into the waxed surface of the tablet.

Sulpicia (*c.* 30 BC)

Although we know that several Roman women wrote poems and letters, very little women's writing has survived. Sulpicia's poetry was kept almost by accident, because it was collected together with the works of a famous male poet, who was one of her friends. Sulpicia came from a wealthy family that gave money to support male writers. She met many of them at her home and learned a great deal about poetry. But her own poems are unlike anything else written at the time. She experimented with using words in different ways—with double meanings and unusual rhythms and rhymes. She wrote passionately about falling in love, and insisted that women's feelings were as strong and important as men's.

Law and Politics

Women in Roman lands had few political rights, and it was almost impossible for them to gain political power. Some women managed to play a part in politics by persuading their husbands or other powerful men to represent them, or by taking part in secret plots and schemes. These were unreliable ways of taking action, and often dangerous. Even so, a few women dared to challenge the rules of Roman society.

Sempronia (c. 63 BC)

Sempronia was born into a noble family, and was a friend and political ally of Catiline, a Roman politician who was accused of plotting against the government. Sempronia's political views were very unpopular, and her enemies accused her of immoral behavior. But she was intelligent and argued brilliantly. Her critics described her as educated, skilled at playing the lyre, and able to dance "more elegantly than was necessary for a respectable woman."

Amasia Sentia (first century AD)

Normally, Roman women did not appear in law courts, unless they were accused of a crime or called as witnesses. But we do know the names of a few Roman women who learned enough about the law, and were confident enough, to conduct their own cases in court. In the first century AD, Amasia Sentia was accused of a crime. Rather than hire a lawyer to defend her, she argued her own innocence. She argued so well that she won her case. But she was criticized by one male writer at the time as having a man's spirit in a woman's body.

Hortensia (first century BC)

In 42 BC the Roman government needed more money to fight a civil war. They demanded that Rome's richest women pay a special war tax. The women were angry and marched into the Forum in Rome—an almost unheard-of event. They chose Hortensia, the daughter of a famous politician, to speak for them. She made a powerful speech, asking why women should give up their property in wartime, when they had already lost their husbands, fathers and sons in battle. She also argued that it was unfair to tax women, because they had no chance to decide government policy. Government leaders tried to arrest Hortensia, but the crowds of people who came to listen to her were so impressed by her courage and arguments that the government leaders changed their minds.

Hortensia led her band of women protesters out of their homes into the Roman Forum, a public place where men met to discuss politics and law.

Boudicca became ruler of the Iceni people after her husband died. Roman writers commented on the tradition of strong women in Celtic lands. They said that when angry, Celtic women were more terrifying than Celtic men.

Boudicca (died AD 62)

Queen Boudicca was the wife of Prasutagus, King of the Iceni people who lived in south-east England. When he died in AD 60, the Romans (who had recently invaded southern Britain) put his relatives in prison or made them slaves. Boudicca joined with another people, the Trinobantes, to attack Roman camps and forts. In AD 61 she marched on London with a large army and left the city in ruins. Roman historians claimed that her troops killed 70,000 Roman soldiers and British people who had accepted Roman rule. Boudicca's army was finally defeated by Roman soldiers, and Boudicca was trapped on the battlefield. She took poison rather than surrender and be captured.

Livia (*c.* 55 BC–AD 29)

Livia gained power through her good looks and her influence on men. She was so beautiful that Emperor Augustus commanded her to divorce her husband so that she could marry him instead. She became devoted to Augustus and acted as his advisor. But she was very ambitious and was soon criticized for meddling in politics. Livia plotted to make Tiberius, one of her sons by her first marriage, emperor. She continued to try and influence the government, until Tiberius moved away from Rome to escape her scheming.

Zenobia (died AD 274)

Zenobia was born in Arabia. She married the king of Syria, a country conquered by Rome. After Zenobia's husband died, she declared that her country was no longer ruled from Rome. People at the time thought that Zenobia had killed her husband because she wanted to rule the country herself. They described her as beautiful, brave and ambitious. Zenobia led her own troops to conquer Egypt and other nearby countries. In AD 272 she was captured by the Romans. They agreed to set her free if she stopped fighting, but recaptured her the following year when she started to fight again. She and her son were taken to Rome, and marched through the streets in chains. Later, she was pardoned, and married a wealthy Roman senator, ending her life peacefully in Rome.

A bronze coin made in about AD 270, showing Queen Zenobia.

GLOSSARY

accounts Records of money earned and spent.

alliance An agreement between friendly peoples or nations.

ancestors Relatives who have died.

ancient Greeks The people who lived in Greece and the nearby lands. Their civilization was most powerful from about 1000 to 200 BC.

aqueduct A raised channel for carrying water.

brothel A house where prostitutes work.

Celts Peoples who lived in central and northern Europe. Their civilization was most powerful from about 800 BC to AD 50.

ceremony A gathering of people, with music and prayers, in honor of a special event.

civil rights The rights that allow a person to play a full part in society, such as having a say in what laws are passed and how the government is run.

civil war A war between different groups in the same country.

civilization A society with its own laws, customs, beliefs and artistic traditions.

commission (in the arts) Paying for something to be specially made.

concubine In Rome, a woman who lived with a man as if she were his wife, but who was not legally married to him.

Church The organization of the Christian religion.

cult A group of people who share the same religious beliefs or religious activities.

culture Beliefs, customs and artistic traditions.

curses Words or thoughts that wish another person bad luck or harm.

customs Established ways of doing things.

dictated Spoken out loud, to be written down by someone else.

dictator A ruler who can override the law. The Romans appointed dictators in times of emergency.

dowry Goods given by a bride's family to her husband on her wedding day.

empire A large area of land, often including many different countries, areas and peoples, governed by the ruler of the strongest one.

estate A very large farm belonging to a single family.

family honor A family's reputation. In Rome, this affected someone's place in society.

flax A tall plant. Its fibers are woven together to make linen cloth.

forum An open space in the center of Roman cities where markets were held and people met to discuss business and politics.

gorgon A bloodthirsty monster from ancient Greek and Roman myths. The gorgon looked like a woman, but had sharp fangs and snakes instead of hair. She could turn people to stone just by looking at them.

guardian A person who is legally responsible for looking after someone else.

guild An organization of people who do the same job, and who help one another.

hearth The fireplace (often used for cooking) at the center of a home.

hostess The senior woman in a household who welcomes guests into her home.

household. Everyone who lives in one home, including parents, children, grandparents, other relatives, servants and slaves.

ideal Perfect in every way. Something to aim for or to measure things against.

immoral Breaking society's laws of good behavior.

incense Something that is burned to give off sweet-smelling smoke. It is often used during religious ceremonies.

inheritance Goods and land passed down from one generation to another.

laundress A woman who makes a living by washing other people's clothes.

law code A collection of laws.

magistrates In Rome, senior lawmakers and heads of government, who also controlled the army.

midwife A trained woman who helps mothers during pregnancy and in childbirth.

monument A building or statue designed to remind everyone of an important person or event.

moral power Power that comes from beliefs about what is right and good.

mosaics Pictures made out of tiny pieces of stone, pottery or glass.

mourner A person who is sad at someone's death. In Rome there were also professional mourners, who were paid to weep and look sad at funerals.

parchment Cleaned sheepskin (with the fleece removed) used by people to write on.

philosophy The study of ideas and beliefs.

policy Plans and aims.

rebellion A war by people against their rulers.

ritual The set form of a ceremony.

sacred Holy, devoted to a god or religious purpose.

sacrifice An offering to the gods.

senator A member of the senior families of Rome. Senators helped make new laws. They were all men.

shrine A holy place.

social reforms Plans to improve the way people live.

taverns Cafés or bars selling food and wine.

tax Money paid by workers and landowners to a government, to help pay for public services, such as the army, law courts and roads.

tomb A place, often like an underground room, where someone is buried. It is often marked with a carved slab, or tombstone.

vow A solemn promise.

wet nurse A woman who breastfeeds another woman's child, for money.

widow A woman whose husband has died.

FURTHER READING

Dr Sarah McNeill, *Ancient Romans at a Glance* (Peter Bedrick Books)

Simon James, *Ancient Rome* (Viking Press)

Judith Simpson, *Ancient Rome* (Nature Company Discoveries Library, Time Life)

Fiona Macdonald, *First Facts About the Ancient Romans* (Peter Bedrick Books)

Louise James, *How We Know About the Romans* (Peter Bedrick Books)

Mike Corbishley, *What Do We Know About the Romans?* (Peter Bedrick Books)

INDEX